Sacrament Time

By
Kathleen H. Barnes
Virginia H. Pearce

Photographs by
Don O. Thorpe

A book for LDS children

Published by Deseret Book Company
Salt Lake City, Utah
1973

Lithographed by
DESERET PRESS
in the United States of America

Mommy and Daddy say that sacrament time is a special time of the week.
They say it's a quiet time to think about Jesus and how much we want to be like Him.

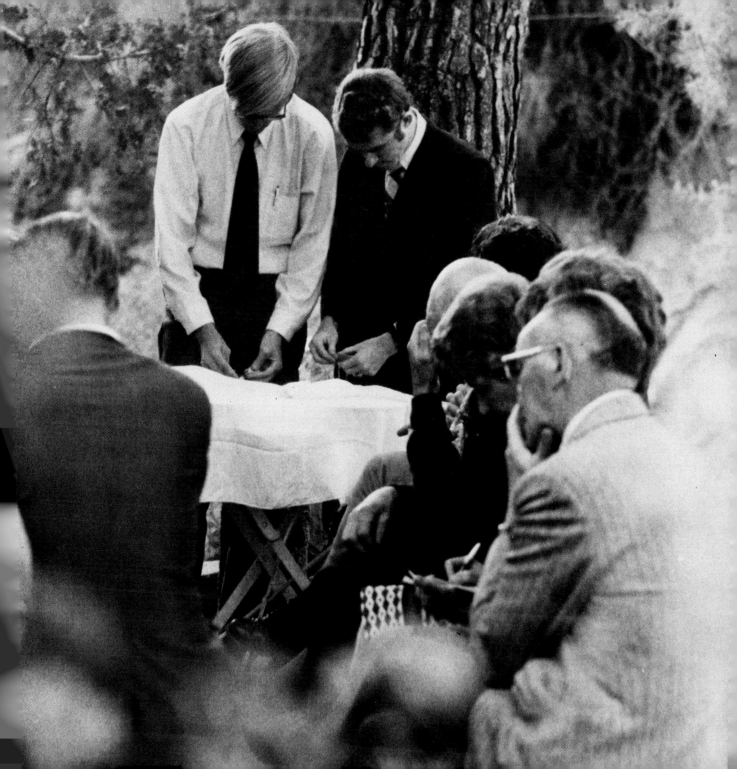

But...
My feet begin to wiggle and
My mouth begins to giggle and
My hands will not be still.

I want to be like Mommy and Daddy.
I want to think about Jesus.
So during sacrament time...

I can think about praying to my Heavenly Father.

Jesus prayed to Heavenly Father.

One night Jesus was very sad. He went into a beautiful garden called Gethsamane. He knelt down and prayed to Heavenly Father.
After He prayed, Jesus knew Heavenly Father would help Him.
Matthew 26:39

I can think about helping
someone who is sad.

Arab woman, Beersheva, Israel

Jesus helped the sad.

One day when Jesus was eating dinner in a man's house a woman came in and stood behind Him. Because this woman had done many things that were wrong the people in the house were not nice to her. She cried because she was so sorry for things that she had done. Jesus forgave her and this made her very happy.

Luke 7:36-50

I can think
about taking care
of someone who
is sick.

Jesus cared for the sick.

One day a very sick man came to Jesus. This man had terrible sores all over his body. The doctors could not help him. Jesus laid his hands on him and blessed him. The man was happy because the sores were healed and he was well again.

Mark 1:40-45

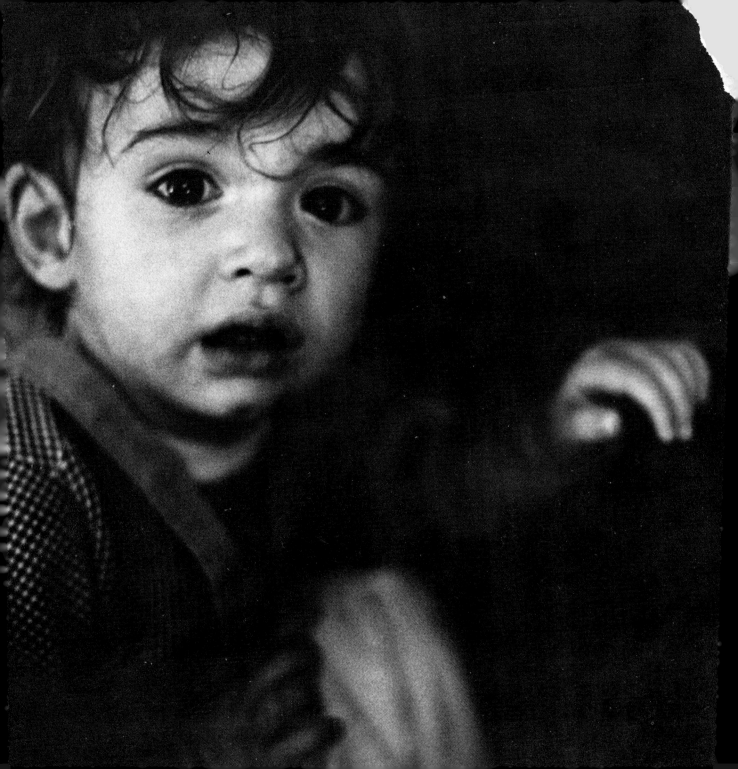

I can think about feeding someone who is hungry.

One day Jesus was talking to a
great crowd of people. They
listened to Him so long that they
grew very hungry. One little boy
had some bread and fishes, but
not enough for so many people.
He gave them to Jesus.
Because Jesus loved the people
and did not want them to be
hungry, He blessed the bread
and fishes. Then He had enough
to feed all of the people.
John 6:5-14

Jesus fed the hungry.

The Western Wall, Jerusalem

I can think about helping someone in trouble.

Rocky stream bed near Shiloh, Israel

There was a woman who had done something wrong. Because of this some men wanted to throw rocks at her. Jesus talked to them quietly and kindly until they put down their rocks and went away.

John 8:1-11

Jesus helped people in trouble.

I can think about obeying the laws of my country.

Jesus obeyed the law.

When Jesus lived on earth, one of the laws of the land was to attend the Feast of the Passover. Jesus often went to Jerusalem with his parents to obey this law.

Luke 2:41

Jerusalem

I can think about loving
my brother and sister.

Arab children in Jerusalem

Jesus loved everyone.

One day Jesus was talking to a crowd of people. The children all wanted to be close to Jesus but the disciples tried to turn them away because they thought Jesus did not have time for them. When Jesus saw the children, He said, "Suffer the little children to come unto me and He took them up in His arms, put His hands upon them, and blessed them."

Mark 10:13-16

If I do all the things that Jesus did,
one day He will put
His arms around me
and bless me and
I will live with Him forever.

And if I think about these things,
Next Sunday, sacrament time
will be a special time
of the week for me…

…And my feet won't wiggle and
My mouth won't giggle and
My hands will be so still, because
I'll be thinking about Jesus
and how I can be like him.